Potty
Training

PRACTICAL™
parenting

Potty Training

Making the transition without
stress or mess

Dr Jane Gilbert

hamlyn

*To Megan and Elin,
who taught me more about
potty training than any
research paper.*

A Pyramid Paperback

First published in Great Britain
in 2003 by Hamlyn, a division of
Octopus Publishing Group Ltd
2–4 Heron Quays,
London E14 4JP

Copyright © Octopus Publishing
Group Ltd 2003, 2006

This material was previously
published as *Potty Training*.

ISBN-13: 978-0-600-61443-2
ISBN-10: 0-600-61443-3

A CIP catalogue record for
this book is available from the
British Library.

Printed and bound in China

10 9 8 7 6 5 4 3 2

contents

Introduction

When you're a new parent, up to your elbows in dirty nappies, the idea of toilet training a child can seem very attractive. Later on, the looming vision of potties, puddles and tantrums can be intimidating.

Above When you're changing a dirty nappy the idea of potty training can seem very appealing.

The very phrase 'potty training' conjures up visions of toddlers lined up on potties, being instructed as if in a military drill. 'Potty learning' might be a better description, but I have decided not to be overly worried about terminology: everyone knows what potty training is, so generally that's the term I've used. The overall tone and approach of the book should (hopefully) make it clear that I'm not advocating marching your toddler to the bathroom every 20 minutes and making her stay there until she's done something.

Pressure from friends and grandparents can make child-rearing feel like a race. It's easy to get tricked into thinking that the 'best' parents have children who walk, talk and wear pants at a very young age. The truth is that they're just normal developmental stages, which can't be hurried. I hope that the information in this book will give you the freedom to choose the right time to try without nappies, without rushing. For me, the moment I first saw my toddlers running away from me in a pair of pants was filled with relief, pride and sadness that they really weren't my little babies any more.

As a doctor, I have advised parents on strategies to entice children out of nappies; as a mum, I mopped floors, sponged sofas and pulled my hair out just like everyone else. In writing this book I have used a combination of medical research, personal experience and advice from parents who have survived potty training and have a child in pants to prove it. I hope that the advice I have provided will relieve some of the stress – and mess – involved in helping your child out of nappies and on to the toilet.

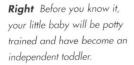

Right *Before you know it, your little baby will be potty trained and have become an independent toddler.*

the right time

1

- Child development

- Girls and boys

- Recognizing the signs

- In my day

- Potty pressure

Child development

It would be so much easier if there were a magic age at which to potty train your child. You could simply wake up on the morning that he reaches, say, 26 months, plonk him on the potty – and hey presto!

However, every child is different. Some gain the necessary physical, mental and emotional developmental skills as early as 18 months, whereas others aren't ready until they're 3 or 4 years old. Some get the hang of it over a weekend, while others take months. By responding to your child's signals you can let him set the agenda, so that you'll both find the transition from nappies to pants as painless as possible.

A series of skills

Weeing or pooing on the potty is a highly complex process. Really, it is. It may not seem very difficult to you, but when you break down the number of skills that are needed to succeed it's incredible that someone as young as a 2- or 3-year-old could ever master it.

- Your toddler has to be able to recognize the signs that he needs to go to the toilet, and then hold on to it long enough to get there.
- He then has to remember where the potty is, walk to it, grapple with his clothing and pull down his pants - and all this before he even sits down to do his business.
- Finally, he needs to wipe his bottom, get dressed and wash his hands.

Ages and stages

In order for a child to succeed, he has to be physically and mentally ready. Scientists have identified a number of stages your child will go through while developing bladder and bowel control:

1 **He becomes aware of having a wet or dirty nappy or clothing.** This can occur from 15 months.

Below *Let your child show you when she's ready to try the potty.*

2 **He recognizes when he is doing a wee or a poo,** and may learn the words to tell you all about it. This takes place between 18 and 24 months, or later in some children.

3 **He can tell you in advance that he will need to go,** with sufficient warning for you to get him to the potty in time. On average, this occurs between 2½ and 3 years.

4 **He gains more control of his bladder and can 'hold on' for a while.** This takes place from 3 years onwards.

Physical maturity

Research has shown that a child cannot voluntarily use the muscles that control his bladder and rectum until he is at least 18 months old. There is a gap of roughly 2 years between the age when a child first starts to recognize that he's wet, and the time when he can actually hold on and wait before he passes urine. Potty training will be faster if your child is at the last stage before you start; although with perseverance you can certainly achieve dryness earlier, it will be a longer, more drawn-out and, probably, messier process.

Above A toddler who is becoming more independent will be keener to start potty training.

Emotional maturity

A child who is physically ready may still not be prepared to let go of her nappies. Motivation is the key, and a toddler who is becoming more independent and keen to do things for herself will be more interested in going to the toilet like a grown-up than a child who is at an earlier stage of her emotional development.

Many children will show strong signs that they are physically, mentally and emotionally ready for potty training before the age of 3. However, at least 15 per cent of children are not potty trained by that age, and 4 per cent still haven't mastered it by 4 years.

It's important not to panic that your child is falling behind. One research study presented at a European conference for bladder and kidney specialists revealed that for healthy children, bladder capacity increases significantly between the ages of 2 and 3 years, so that by the time they are 3 most children are able to hold on and stay dry for longer periods of time. Your child will get there, in her own time.

More haste, less speed

In the USA, paediatricians have a saying about potty training:

'If you start at 2, you'll be done by 3.
If you start at 3, you'll be done by 3!'

Girls and boys

Research is now confirming what parents have known for years:
that boys tend to be a little slower to gain control of their bladders
and bowels than girls. One study showed that, on average, boys
both started and completed potty training later than girls.

According to American research, the average age
for completion of potty training (day and night-time
dryness) was 35 months for girls and 39 months
for boys. This difference is thought to be due to
several factors:

1 Boys' nervous systems mature later.
Girls can begin to gain bladder control from the
age of 18 months, whereas with boys it may not be
until after 22 months.

2 Women still tend to be the main carers,
so boys do not see a same-sex role model as
often as girls do.

**3 Boys appear to be less
sensitive to the feeling
of wetness against
their skin.** But don't
get bogged down in
the detail. Every child
is different, and if your
son seems ready then
you should go for it,
whatever his age.

'Everyone had always said that
boys are slower, and in my
experience that's probably true. I
waited much longer before potty
training Tom; he was over 2½. In
the end it was really easy, he just
about trained himself.'

*Sandra, mother of Laura (7)
and Tom (4)*

*Right Boys tend to be a little slower to
learn toileting.*

Recognizing the signs

Most children will show characteristic signs when they are ready to take on potty training – you just have to be able to recognize these and act on them. If that sounds too much like taking part in a complicated detection exercise, take heart from the fact that some children, especially those with older siblings, can make it very easy for you.

My second daughter simply pulled off her nappy at 20 months and refused point blank to wear one again, because she wasn't a baby. She knew she was ready; I wasn't so sure, especially after changing her 'big girl pants' for the hundredth time. She refused to give in to my pleadings to put her nappy back on, and eventually we succeeded.

Below *A child who is ready will be able to pull his pants up and down.*

Is your child ready?

Many children's signals are subtler than my daughter's were. Although there isn't a checklist you should tick off, there is a gradual accumulation of indicators that your child is becoming physically, mentally and emotionally ready to learn to go to the toilet. Your child may be ready to start toilet training if:

- **'I can do it' becomes a regular refrain,** showing that your toddler wants to become more independent.
- **He has regular, formed bowel movements,** and he may go red in the face and gain a very concentrated expression when he's about to go.
- **He has the dexterity to pull his pants up and down by himself.**

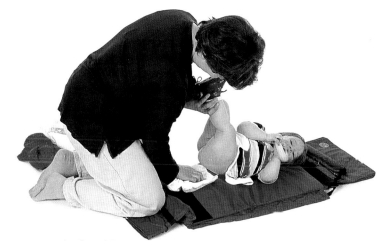

- **He's very interested when his father goes to the toilet** and imitates his actions.
- **He is developed physically** so that he can walk and sit down on the potty.
- **He knows what wee and poo are** and may talk about them when you're changing his nappy.
- **You may notice that his nappy is dry for longer periods,** up to three or four hours. This shows that his bladder capacity and control are improving.
- **He can understand what you are saying and follow simple instructions,** such as 'Go and get your teddy.'
- **He starts to recognize the sensations that he needs to go to the toilet** and demonstrates this by looking uncomfortable, holding onto himself or grunting. Soon he'll learn to tell you before it happens.
- **He may become uncomfortable and complain if his nappy is dirty.**
- **He may start to rip off his nappy every time he does a wee in it,** which means he can go through ten nappies a day. If this is the case, simple economics dictate that it's time to reach for the potty.

Above *You may notice that your child's nappies are dry after three or four hours.*

15

In my day

Potty-training practices have changed considerably over the years. Mothers from previous generations were encouraged to start extraordinarily early, and it was not unheard of to balance babies on the potty as soon as they could sit up, or even earlier.

Things have certainly improved in recent years. However, a lot of parents come under pressure from their own parents and grandparents to 'get on with it', as if early dryness were a badge of honour and having a child in nappies a sign of laziness.

No need to rush

It's true that we have become much more relaxed about potty training: partly because we know far more about children's development and how their bodily control matures, and partly because disposable nappies have made life so much easier that there simply isn't the incentive to rush. And what would you be rushing for? It isn't going to make your child cleverer or happier. It is much better to let her lead the way and learn to use the potty or toilet when she is ready.

'My mum really put pressure on me to potty train my children. She made no secret of disapproving of my relaxed attitude. She used to tut and shake her head when she saw their nappies. She made me feel terribly guilty. I tried just to ignore it – but it's so difficult and I probably started toilet training earlier than I'd have liked because of her.'

Vanessa, mother of Harry (6) and Jack (4)

'With terry nappies, especially as your child got older, they were saturated after one wee. I was constantly washing, so we were definitely encouraged to get on with potty training as early as possible.'

Jan, mother of Jane (34) and Justin (32)

Right Older generations may see early potty training as a badge of honour.

In the past

During the 19th century, dangling tiny infants over a potty was regularly practised. Parenting books of the day advised mothers to get rid of cloth nappies after the first few months. Pye Henry Chavasse's Advice to a Mother (1880) advocated that:

A babe of three months and upwards, ought to be held out, at least a dozen times during the twenty-four hours. If such a plan were adopted, napkins might, at the end of three months be dispensed with – a great desideratum – and he would be inducted into clean habits – a blessing to himself, and a comfort to all around, and a great saving of dresses and of furniture.

Potty pressure

Parents boast about their kids – even those who complain about their child's behaviour are bragging in a 'my child is naughtier than your child' way. It starts with birth weights and apgar scores and continues through first smiles, 'mamas' and 'dadas', and physical milestones. When it comes to potty training, the social pressure to rush can be intense: even the most laid-back parent may compare their child with those of their peers.

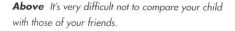

Above *It's very difficult not to compare your child with those of your friends.*

'My first son hadn't shown any signs of being ready to potty train by 2 years 8 months. All my friends' kids were out of nappies, even though some of them were much younger than him, and I felt terrible. I really thought I was a useless mum because I couldn't get him dry, and I kept on trying to force him onto the potty. Eventually it became so stressful that I just gave up, and when he was 3 he went on the potty himself one day. We haven't had any accidents since. With my second boy I was much more relaxed and didn't even try until he was approaching 3, and the whole process was calm and straightforward. They're both bright little boys. I wish I'd known how unimportant it is to train them early: we'd have had a lot less stress and a lot more fun.'

Yvonne, mother of Sam (6) and Benedict (4)

When everyone else's child has apparently been potty trained since the age of 18 months and is now dry by night, while yours will sit happily in a smelly nappy for hours on end, it's difficult not to panic.

You can't hurry nature

But potty training is not a race. One research study concluded that 'development of bladder and bowel control is largely a maturational process which cannot be accelerated by an early onset or a high intensity of training.' In other words, your child will do it when he is ready, not when you are. The researchers also found that age of toilet training wasn't affected by premature birth (although age should still be corrected, to take account of the prematurity), problems around the perinatal period and even mild to moderate neurological impairment.

You can reassure yourself that really happy, intelligent and well-adjusted children (with lovely, competent parents!) may have been toilet trained at a late age – it doesn't matter.

potty
preparation

2

Show them the way

As with so much in life, preparation is everything. The toilet learning process should start a long time before you put your toddler in a pair of pants and place her on a potty. I'm not talking about a campaign of military precision, just a gradual introduction to the whole idea of going to the toilet like a grown-up.

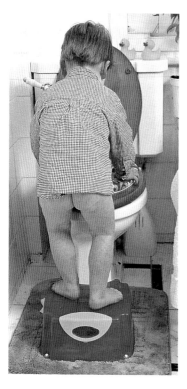

Above Children like to copy the grown ups. A daddy or big brother can demonstrate the advanced standing technique.

If you take your time and make sure your child understands what it's all about before you start, then potty training can be relatively stress, and mess, free.

A toddler is rarely far from your side. Whether you're getting dressed, having a bath or going to the toilet, you can be sure she'll be right next to you, watching intently. Now is the time to make the most of her interest. Although you'd probably prefer to lock the bathroom door and get some peace and quiet, you can take advantage of the situation and make your child interested in using the toilet by showing her the way.

Learning by imitation

Children are wonderful mimics. By watching mum and dad on the toilet, they imitate and learn. You've probably already noticed your child copying you or repeating one of your more choice expletives, so exploit that ability. Explain what you're doing when you go to the toilet – she'll love all the gory details. If your toddler is a boy, his father can volunteer to demonstrate the standing technique. There are several other strategies you can employ:

- **It's never too soon to start.** Show your child how to wipe from front to back and flush the paper away. Allow her to pull the flush – some children

may be inspired to repeat the action a hundred times a day. You may find your patience being severely tested, but kids can be frightened by the loud noise and splashing, so anything that makes toileting familiar and fun will help.

Above *Let your child get to know his potty – but make sure you've disinfected it first!*

- **Putting a potty in the bathroom may stir your child's interest.** Don't expect miracles: it's unlikely that she is going sit down and perform perfectly immediately. She'll probably explore the potty and use it as a plaything, or even a hat! That's fine – when she's ready to be trained, the toilet and potty won't be scary or intimidating.

- **A dolly or teddy could demonstrate what the potty is really for.** If you can find a doll that actually wees, your child will be intrigued to see the potential result of potty sitting.

- **Older siblings and friends can also set a great example.** Let your toddler watch them using the toilet or potty and she'll be keener to try it out herself.

I done a wee-wee

Anyone who has ever spent five minutes in a school playground will be aware that children love discussing poos, wee and bottoms. The mere mention of the words will cause them to collapse into giggles. You may not be overly keen to trigger this fascination with bodily functions in your toddler. However, being aware is the first stage in getting ready to potty train.

When you're changing your child's nappy, comment on how wet it is. If he does a wee or (if you're very unlucky) a poo in the bath, describe what's happened – while quickly getting him out of the bath and reaching for the disinfectant!

With time, he'll start to notice that his body produces strange liquids and solids, and may recognize the sensations he feels as they're being passed. If you notice the characteristic signs – becoming quiet, going red and concentrating – that your child is about to do a poo, then you could calmly tell him that you think this is going to happen. If it's warm and he's running around outside, take off his nappy and he will become more aware of his body and all its functions.

What's in a name?

Wee, pee, urine, poo, poop: the words you choose to use are entirely up to you. Be sure you're comfortable with the terms you've chosen, because

Left Kids love to talk about wees and poos. The very mention of the words will have giggling.

Right *Talk to your child so that she's more aware of her body's functions.*

you'll be hearing them an awful lot over the next few months. It's also sensible to choose words that you're happy using in public. Kids are endearingly up front about going to the toilet, and you may well find your child announcing to an entire restaurant that he's 'done a big poo-poo'.

It also helps if you use the same words all the time: you may know ten different words for urine but your child won't, and if you start talking about pee when he's used to wee, he may think you're talking about a whole different subject.

'Some friends of ours decided to be very up front and biological with their children. They were taught, as soon as they could talk, to use the words penis and vagina. But pretty soon the kids had improved on the scientific terms and were talking about their peanut and angina! I think there's definitely an argument forchoosing a child-friendly word that all their friends will also be using.'

Ann, mother of Sarah (34) and David (32)

Real pants or nappy pants?

At first, nappy pants seemed to be the answer to potty-training problems: no mess, no dirty pants, and less stress for parent and toddler. Then, rumblings passed from parent to parent like jungle drums that they could cause problems.

Above Nappy pants can make life easier – and cleaner – in the early days of potty training.

The argument was that children find it difficult to differentiate between nappy pants and nappies, and can wee to their heart's content without getting wet and uncomfortable – so what's the incentive to use the potty? It was claimed that using nappy pants could prolong the potty-training process. Big girl (or big boy) pants are quite different: if you wee in those, you, your parent and the carpet really know about it.

The choice is yours

The truth is that it is a matter of personal choice. Potty training may take longer with nappy pants, but it may also be a much calmer, cleaner and more pleasant experience for both parent and child. You may find that nappy pants are useful for early outings or car journeys. They also help to bridge the gap between nappies and real pants when your toddler is still having frequent accidents.

However, it is vital that you treat them as 'real' pants. It's no good saying 'Go on, wee in your nappy pants this time,' just because you're out shopping and it's inconvenient to stop and go for a wee for the twentieth time. Consistency is everything, and although it is utterly infuriating being with a newly trained toddler, it will be more infuriating if your mixed messages drag out the whole process for even longer.

The choice is hers

You can make your toddler excited about the potty-training process by taking her out to choose her own pants. With a brand new pair of pants sporting pictures of her favourite cartoon character, she'll feel very grown up and proud, and hopefully less inclined to sully them with an accident.

Ask the expert

'Many parents tell me that children tend to see nappy pants as the same as nappies. I believe that if a child is showing all the signals that they're ready, it's better to go for it and use pants.'

Vivien Alderson, health visitor

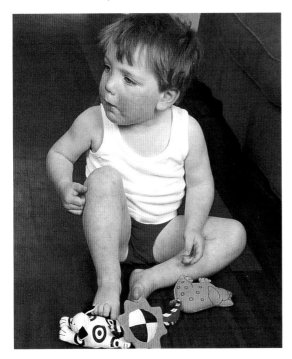

Left Let your child choose his own big-boy pants.

What potty?

There's a bewildering array of potties on the shelves, from simple pots to throne-like devices with sound and light shows. I'm a great believer in quantity over quality when it comes to potties: the more you have, the shorter the running distance to get your toddler onto it when nature calls.

Also, by leaving potties all around the house you increase the chances that your child will happen upon one when he feels the urge, and go on it under his own steam. Try begging or borrowing potties from friends with older children, so that there's always one in or near the rooms you use most.

You could also take your toddler shopping for the potty that appeals to him: if he likes it, he's more likely to sit on it. It's a fact of life that a toddler is unlikely to choose something that matches your bathroom colour scheme, but in this case practicality should take precedence over interior design.

The main options are:

- **One-piece potty.** These are cheap, cheerful and perfectly functional, although they aren't as widely stocked as they used to be. You may inherit one from a friend whose children are older. They are low and easy to get onto for small toddlers, although older children may struggle. These potties are lightweight, so can be taken on outings. The problem is that your child may cause a mess if he likes to empty the potty into the toilet himself, as they can be rather cumbersome. A potty of this type is also so light and portable that your little one may be tempted to race around the floor on it!

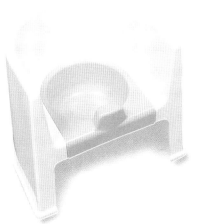

● **Potty with removable cup.** These are bigger, which makes them rather popular with impressionable toddlers. They have a central cup which can be removed, making emptying and cleaning easier for parents and older children. They are lightweight, but probably a bit big to use on outings. Some models have lids to minimize splashing when emptying.

● **High-tech potty.** More and more manufacturers are designing potties with a range of gadgets. They may have integral toilet-roll holders, storage for books, and buttons to press to make the potty 'sing'. I have even read about a prototype potty on which you can pre-record your voice; then, when your child wees in the potty a sensor triggers it to play your voice saying: 'Who's a clever girl?' or any other suitable encouragement.

If it works for you and catches the imagination of your toddler, fine, but do be careful that you're not spending money on something your child will love to play with but isn't the least bit interested in using for its intended function.

Straight to the toilet

The term 'potty training' suggests that a potty is an essential part of the process. However lots of families find it easier to go straight from nappies to the toilet, leaving out the middleman.

Above Lots of children prefer to go straight from nappies to the toilet.

'I hate emptying dirty potties and so we encouraged Jessica to do a poo on the toilet from the very beginning. We bought a special seat to make it more comfortable for her. It worked really well, she's happy and I don't have to clean out the potty!'

Deborah, mother of Jessica (2¾)

In many ways it makes perfect sense; your toddler will already be accustomed to seeing the toilet, having no doubt followed you to the bathroom for months! This means that for some children it can seem much more natural to wee on the toilet like mum and dad.

Pros
- No cleaning out of dirty potties.
- You don't have to negotiate the transition from potty to toilet.
- It's cheaper; you already have a toilet and the adaptor ring will last until they're big enough to sit on the toilet alone.
- For toddlers it can seem more grown up to use a toilet just like mummy and daddy.

Cons
- Children may find a toilet intimidating and frightening.
- You have to find a toilet on early outings and can't just pull out your potty.
- You can scatter potties all around the house so that they can wee if the mood takes them, the toilet is likely to be further away so there may be more early accidents.

toilet tips

If you'd like your toddler to give potties a miss and go straight to the toilet, here are a few ways to make life easier.

1 **Follow the leader**. Take them with you when you go to the toilet and get them used to sitting on the seat with their nappy on. When it's time for toilet training, it will already seem safe and familiar.

2 **Adapt your toilet.** An adaptor ring is a cost-effective way of using your own toilet for potty training. It should sit safely on top of the loo seat and as well as being more comfortable it will stop their little bottoms from slipping into the toilet bowl.

3 **Step up to it.** Make sure you also buy a sturdy step so that they can get up themselves. There are enough jobs for parents to do, without always having to lift your child on and off the toilet. Especially as you're likely to be required to do so every five minutes in the early days. The step will also provide a safe base to plant their feet, so they'll feel safer while they sit.

4 **Keep it clean.** Toddlers will use their hands to balance on the toilet seat, so make sure it is kept clean and disinfected. Encourage them into good habits by teaching them to wash their hands, using the step to stand on.

5 **Don't push.** For some toddlers the big toilet can seem frightening, with its' loud noises and splashing. Even with a booster seat they may worry they'll fall down and get flushed away! If your child isn't keen, use the potty instead, or try some of the tips in on page 70.

Above *You can buy a step to help your child get up onto the toilet herself.*

Childcare

For a parent who is at home full-time, the idea of handing over a potty-training toddler to another carer during the day can seem extremely appealing – there is someone else to mop up the floor and take some of the strain. But working parents often worry that by 'letting go' of their child, all the progress they made with the potty over the weekend will be undone.

The good news for working parents is that researchers have found no difference in children's toilet training whether they had working parents and were in full-time daycare, or were cared for at home. 'Our findings should provide reassurance to working parents. It's important that parents realize potty training is not an overnight process, instead it takes around 8 to 10 months and that usually includes some stops and starts,' says Dr Schum, who carried out the research. 'Parents should be patient and offer children as much positive support as possible throughout this process.'

Tips for success

You can make life easier for yourself and your toddler who is at nursery by making use of the following tips (most of which also apply if your child is being cared for by a childminder):

● **Talk about it.** Before you embark on the potty-training process, it is worth talking through the nursery's policy with staff. It's essential that you know what they are planning and that they understand your feelings and preferences for your child.

Above *Research shows that children in childcare are potty trained at the same times as those who are cared for at home.*

Questions you might like to ask include:

- When do they like to potty train?
- Do they prefer children to be in nappy pants or real pants?
- Will your child have a special carer who will support him and spot if he may need to use the potty?
- Where do they keep the potties?
- What do they do if a child has an accident?
- Will you be able to talk daily to someone about how things have gone?

- **Be prepared.** Let the nursery know as soon as you're starting to think about potty training. They can help you to identify clues that your child is ready, and they can also assist in making your little one familiar with the potty. Toddlers in childcare are at an advantage, because there are usually lots of other children around who have either just learned or are learning to use the potty. By watching his friends, your toddler will soon get the hang of what he's supposed to do. He may also be keen to be 'grown up' and go to the toilet like all the big boys at the nursery.

Above *Talk to the nursery about their policies so that your child is given consistent messages.*

- **Aim for consistency.** Potty training is a shared job and it's important that your child gets the same message at home and at nursery. Communication is the key: make sure the childcare staff know what you're doing at home and vice versa. If all the children at nursery go for a wee and wash their hands before lunch, then it will help if you continue that routine at weekends.

  Similarly, it will assist the staff if you try to engender a little independence in your child. You may have fewer accidents if you spot that your child needs to go, carry her to the potty, pull down her pants and wipe her bottom, but this is unlikely to be practical in the nursery environment – and, let's face it, not terribly convenient at home – so encourage her to do things for herself and then praise her if she succeeds.

Below Your child will learn by watching and imitating her friends.

Provide plenty of changes of clothes.
Many parents will know the stab of
disappointment when you turn up at the nursery
to find your child looking like a street urchin,
dressed in a ramshackle assortment of clashing
clothes at pick-up time. It is a sure sign that she
has had a spectacularly unsuccessful day at potty
training, working her way through the entire bag
of clothes that you provided, and has eventually
been attired in items from the nursery's
emergency wardrobe. Don't put yourself, or your
child, through this. Instead, pack so many
changes of clothes that there are always enough
for any eventuality.

Above Young toddlers in childcare love
to do things like the big children.

'My first daughter went to a nursery where they had a very aggressive policy on potty training. By 2 years of age she was put in pants, even though she didn't seem ready. She regularly had accidents, and even if she did make it to the potty she'd often had a little dribble in her pants first. She became so used to being wet that it really didn't bother her, and it took until she was 3 for her to become reliably dry – she still has the odd accident now. Sophie, my younger girl, went to a different nursery with a relaxed approach. They encouraged her to look at the other kids on their potties, but we only agreed to start putting her in pants when she asked to, at about 2½. She was totally confident about using the potty after a week or so and we've had no problems since.'

Annabel, mother of Emily (5) and Sophie (3)

Above *Try not to blame your child – or the nursery – if you are greeted with a big bag of dirty clothes when you collect him at the end of the day.*

• **Try not to blame.** It can be very upsetting to find a carrier bag full of smelly clothes hanging on your child's hook at nursery. It's tempting to blame the nursery because 'she never has accidents at home'. However, before you storm in with all guns blazing to accuse the nursery of neglecting your child, make sure you are being fair.

Monitor how many accidents she has at home, then go to the nursery and see if you and the staff can work out together what's going wrong. Remember that there's something particularly graphic about having all the accidents clearly shown in dirty clothes at the end of the day. At home it's much easier to forget little puddles on the kitchen floor when she wasn't wearing any pants, or if the dirty clothes get thrown straight into the washing machine.

• **Sew on name tapes.** There will be accidents, and the nursery staff are unlikely to be able to remember which child was wearing which trousers, so make it easy for them and prevent your child's clothes going missing by labelling them all clearly.

Books and videos

Stories and videos can be a good way to introduce your child gently to the whole idea of potties. There are lots of titles around, which will enable your toddler to learn the ins and outs of toilet training in an amusing and entertaining way.

Very few toddlers would listen to you lecturing on the subject of what potties are and what they should be used for, but throw in a few colourful illustrations and cute characters and your child will be putty in your hands. And even if he doesn't show an interest in trying the potty for himself, you will both still enjoy the engaging stories!

'Santa put a potty and a copy of a popular potty book in my 20-month-old daughter's Christmas stocking. She thought it was incredibly grown up and adored the story. We didn't start potty training for another 6 months, but by then she was familiar with the potty and used to shout "POTTY" every time she wanted a wee.'

Elizabeth, mother of Megan (3)

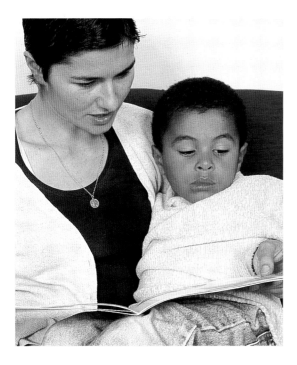

Left *Story-time can be a great introduction into the world of potties.*

nappies off

3

- Make it easy on yourself
- Sense over style
- Now, mummy, now!
- Little boys
- Any time, any place, anywhere
- Cuddles and compliments
- Now wash your hands
- Top 10 mistakes – and how to avoid them

Make it easy on yourself

After all the preparation, it's time to get on with potty training your child. She should already be familiar with the potty and may be keen to try out the pants she has chosen. So if you're ready, then it's nappies off!

Above Wooden floors that wipe clean are great for all those little accidents.

Choose a time when you and your toddler can give potty training a good deal of your attention. It's worth delaying if there's about to be a major upheaval in your lives such as a house move, a change of nursery or a new baby. It's also sensible to put it off if either of you is feeling unwell or recovering from an illness – your child won't perform if she's under the weather, and you may find it harder to cope with those little puddles!

Potty training is a natural part of life and you may feel that it should just fit in with normal activities. In many ways this is true, but you can make things an awful lot easier for yourself by making a few adjustments to your home and routine.

Ideal home

The perfect house for potty training has smooth tiled floors and no soft furnishings: if an accident happens, you can just swill it down and mop it up! I'm not advocating turning your home into a minimalist masterpiece just to make the potty-training process easier. However, it does make sense to make a few alterations to minimize the impact of the puddles that will inevitably occur.

If you have precious rugs or cushions, tidy them away for the next few weeks. Your child won't be able to choose the place where she has an accident, but undoubtedly it will be on your favourite item or the one that is most difficult to clean. If you scold and shout at her, she won't understand the intricacies of the situation: she'll simply feel bad because she had an accident and you were cross. Play in parts of the house, or on pieces of furniture, that are more toddler-proof. In the summer months, the garden is a wonderful place to practise bladder control.

Know your limitations

If you and your toddler have a packed timetable of activities, it's sensible to review them. Although it's good to keep busy, in the early days of potty training you may be setting yourselves too many challenges.

What goes in must come out

Try to ensure that your toddler's diet encourages regular, soft bowel motions. Many 2- and 3- year-olds turn up their noses at the very mention of a vegetable, but baked beans, wholegrain cereals, fruit and plenty of fluids will keep them regular and prevent painful constipation.

Left On warm summer days the garden is the perfect place to experiment without nappies.

Sense over style

Potty training is not the time for designer outfits. Speed is everything in the early days: when your toddler says he wants to go, he *really* wants to go – *now*. Fiddling with tricky buttons, buckles and bows can be the difference between making it and getting caught short. It's very frustrating for your child if he's done his bit and said he wants to go, but he still doesn't manage to wee on the potty.

'I was so proud when Millie first came out of nappies that I really wanted to show her off! Little dresses and tights look so cute without a bulky nappy underneath. Unfortunately, by the time we got to playgroup Millie already needed a wee and was wriggling, so it was difficult to grapple with her tights and pants. She lasted a total of 15 minutes in her beautiful outfit. I left it another month before I risked her in tights again.'

Victoria, mother of Millie (5)

If you've always dressed your toddler to impress, for a while you'll have to put up with lower sartorial standards or just shut your eyes. Choose clothes that allow easy access – stretchy leggings or tracksuit bottoms are perfect. Remember that you may get through several changes of clothes each day, so choose items that can be chucked in the washing machine time and time again.

During the summer months your child will need fewer bulky layers of clothing, which means less struggling to undress and, even better, less washing. On sunny days, you can let your toddler run around the garden with little on, which is fun for him and can be a hassle-free way of kicking off the potty-training process.

Opposite *In the early days, choose clothes that are easy to pull down rather than clothes with difficult buckles and buttons.*

Clothes for potty-training toddlers

OUT

- Dungarees.
- All-in-ones.
- Poppers that do up under the crotch.
- Hand-wash garments or (heaven forbid) anything marked 'dry-clean only'.

IN

- Stretchy leggings.
- Elasticated-waist trousers.
- Skirts and dresses without tights.
- Bare bottoms, especially in the summer when children can run around with nothing on.

Now, mummy, now!

This is where I am supposed to say that potty training is simple, and that if you follow steps A, B and C religiously you'll have no problems. Unfortunately, there isn't a totally right or wrong way to go about potty training.

Above *If you are following the relaxed approach then let her play with her nappy off for a little while.*

However, having spoken to hundreds of parents and reviewed what the experts suggest, it appears that broadly there are two contrasting approaches you should consider. Both are tried and tested and can be equally successful. The right choice for you and your toddler really depends on your personalities and lifestyle.

Taking it easy: the relaxed approach

This method allows potty training to fit in with your normal lifestyle. While you're at home you use pants and potties, but when out and about you use nappies or nappy pants.

This approach may suit you if your child is young, or you'd prefer to continue your normal activities, or if you're laid back about the idea of potty training and you don't mind how long the whole process will take.

What to do

Start gradually by taking off your child's nappy and popping her on the potty for a short time every day. After a meal is a good time to try this, because the bowel is often stimulated to pass a motion when the stomach is distended after food, so the chances of 'catching something' in the pottty are greater.

Left A story may encourage your toddler to sit on the potty for a little longer.

2 If she's not happy to sit still, don't worry and don't force her. You may be able to entice her to stay still a little longer by reading a story or looking at some pictures together.

3 Don't panic if nothing happens; you could leave her playing for a little while with her nappy off. Make sure there's always a potty to hand if she does get the urge.

4 If she does do anything on the potty, give her a cuddle and let her know she's done very well. If she doesn't quite make it in time, try not to scold – just clean it up and tell her that next time it would be brilliant if she made it to the potty.

'I'd really got myself into a state by rushing to potty train William. With Olivia I was much more relaxed. The potty was around if she ever wanted to try it, but she always wore nappies when we were in the car or on an outing. Over a few months the nappies got drier and for short trips she'd wear pants. The change to wearing pants all the time was so gradual we both hardly noticed it. It was just so easy, I wish I'd done the same first time around.'

Annabel, mother of William (6) and Olivia (4)

5 Gradually increase the time your child spends without nappies over the next few weeks and introduce pants while you're at home. You may need to give her a hand with pulling them up and down in the early days, and don't be afraid to leave her without them if the weather's warm.

6 If it seems like a long time since she last went, gently remind her that it may be time for a wee. She's new to this and may forget if she's engrossed in a game.

7 On outings you can use nappies or training pants, but it's a good idea to take a potty as well. If your child does say he wants to go on the potty let him, even if he's wearing a nappy. He's learning to recognize his body's signals and there could be a few false alarms, which may try your patience. Try to grin and bear it: the end is in sight.

Above *Nappy pants can be a real help for early outings.*

8 When he's confident using his potty at home and his nappy has been dry when you've been out, it's time to bite on the bullet and venture out with him in pants. Keep a potty close at hand for emergency wee-stops, and feel proud – you've done it!

The good news
- Your child feels under less pressure.
- You can get on with life as usual and don't have to devote your time to potty training.

The bad news
- It takes longer.
- It's tempting to be lazy and leave your child to wee in nappies when it's difficult to get to a toilet.
- It can be confusing for your child.

Getting on with it: the crash course

This method aims to get all the mess and stress over in one short, sharp burst. Potty training becomes your life. You batten down the hatches and stay in and around the house for a week or so.

The fast-track approach will suit you if your child is older and showing lots of signs that he's really ready to use the potty. You also need to be able to alter your life so that you can devote a whole week or more to staying at home and concentrating on potty training. If you get bored being in one place for long periods, or you're not sure whether your child is quite ready, then this is not the method for you.

'When I potty trained Laura, I just cancelled everything for a week and didn't go anywhere. I think I just didn't want to put too much pressure on her or me. It worked really well and was definitely the best method for us.'

Sandra, mother of Laura (7) and Tom (4)

What to do

1 Choose a time when you can clear your diary and devote yourself to cracking this whole potty-training business.

2 You should already have introduced your toddler to the potty, using some of the techniques described in chapter 2. Now is the time to bring out the grown-up pants and explain that today he's going to start using the potty like a big boy.

3 Put potties around the house and encourage him to sit on one if he needs a wee or poo. Congratulate any successes – and try to clean away any puddles with a smile!

Right *Potty training is a complicated process for your child, so remember to applaud all his successes.*

'Ellie had been showing a few signs that she might be ready to try the potty. She'd done a wee in the bath and was delighted to point it out to everyone, and I'd noticed that her nappies were sometimes quite dry when I changed them. Her sister developed chickenpox, and as it was the summer holidays no one wanted to see us and we were housebound. I used the time to potty train Ellie. It was brilliant, and there was very little stress because we were at home all the time. It was boring, but it was definitely worth it – by the time that her sister was no longer infectious, Ellie was potty trained.'

Liz, mother of Ellie (3½) and India (2½)

4 If you do go out, say that you're going for a wee and encourage your child to sit on the potty too 'just in case'. Take a potty and a change of clothes with you. Be consistent: nappies are for naps and night-time only.

5 If you've timed it right, you'll probably find that after a few days your child will be getting the hang of things and seeking out the potty on her own. You may even discover the odd 'surprise' that she's left to fester in a potty without telling you! Now it's time to start going further afield with your brilliant, toilet-trained toddler – but always with a potty and clean clothes just in case.

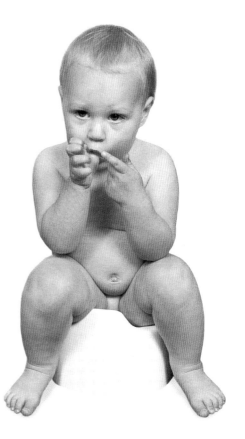

Right *Congratulate yourself – you've done it! Your child has learnt to use the potty.*

6 If things aren't going well after a few days, your toddler is still struggling or you're at breaking point, take a break. Reassure her that she's done very well for her first time, and that next time you know she'll do even better. You can both try again in a month or so.

Above *Remember to check the potties – he may leave a little offering to surprise you!*

The good news
- It's quick.
- Your child gets clear messages about where to wee and when.

The bad news
- It can be messy.
- You may both go 'stir crazy' if you're cooped up at home for a long period.

Little boys

There is an obvious physical difference between boys and girls, and this becomes especially evident during potty training. Perhaps because the main 'toilet trainers' are often women, everything can seem more complicated with boys. Should they sit or stand? Is it better to use the toilet or a potty? And how on earth do you get them to aim where they should and not sprinkle it all over the bathroom?

At the beginning, wee and poo tend to come out at the same time, so it makes sense for your toddler to sit on the potty (or on an adaptor ring on the toilet) for both. He'll be able to learn that they both need to go into the potty, and the whole exciting prospect of having a built-in water cannon won't distract him from the job at hand.

Potties often come with a lip at the front. This is a urine splashguard to stop everything spraying out of the front of the potty and all over your carpet. They're great for protecting your floor covering, but can scrape the penis if your child isn't careful sitting down. So, either teach your son to be cautious, or put up with the odd stray splash.

When your little boy has mastered the idea of sitting down to wee and poo and has gained more control over which he is going to do, it is time to introduce the advanced standing technique.

Left In the beginning it's easier to learn by sitting on the potty.

Tips to help boys hit the target

- **Follow the leader.** A little boy will be more interested in standing up to do a wee if he's seen a 'big boy', father or uncle doing it first.

- **On the level.** Learning to aim successfully is not easy, especially when your little boy's hips may be below the level of the toilet rim. Make it easier for him by putting a sturdy step or stool in the bathroom.

- **Keep it safe.** Make sure the toilet lid or seat can't fall down on your child. If his penis gets caught under a falling seat it will be incredibly painful, and you will need extraordinary powers of persuasion to encourage him to try again.

- **Aim and fire.** Encourage your son to angle his penis down to prevent the entire bathroom being sprayed.

- **Target practice.** Make training fun by turning it into a game. Float torn-up bits of toilet paper or even sprinkle breakfast cereal in the toilet and encourage your son to sink the 'battleships' when he goes for a wee.

- **A splash of colour.** Use a blue food colouring in the toilet. As your son wees into the blue-tinted water, the yellow of the urine will turn the water green. This will (hopefully) encourage him to aim into the pan and not around the room.

- **Keep it clean.** Encourage your son to wipe away any stray splashes with toilet paper and then wash his hands.

- **Put the seat down afterwards.** It's never to early to teach good habits – you can start with this one as soon as he learns to use the toilet.

Above *Once your little boy has mastered sitting on the potty, or toilet, it is time to teach him the standing technique.*

51

Anytime, anyplace, anywhere

Whether you have decided on the intensive, home-based approach to potty training or the more relaxed style, you are eventually going to have to venture out of the house with your toddler. The first time you do this it can feel as if you're an action hero carrying a ticking time bomb, about to go off at any moment!

With time, you will become an expert at toilet spotting, and I've had many conversations with fellow parents about clean and convenient toilet-stops around town. If you can't see a public toilet you can always throw yourself on the shop assistant's mercy – those who are parents tend to be sympathetic, but I have found myself on occasion asking less helpful assistants through clenched teeth whether they'd prefer my daughter to wee on their floor. In general, most supermarkets and large children's stores have toilet facilities.

At the very beginning, it's sensible to have a potty to hand at all times. You may feel like a bag lady weighed down with all the equipment, but as a parent you'll no doubt be used to wandering around laden like a packhorse.

You probably thought life would get easier and your changing bag would become lighter once your child was out of nappies. This may eventually be true, but in the early days you'll need much, much more.

The essential emergency kit

- **Potty.** A portable potty is lightweight and convenient, but make sure your child is familiar with it. A busy pavement with lots of people walking past is not a good time to discover that your daughter will only sit on pink potties.

- **Baby wipes and toilet roll,** with which to wipe bottoms and hands.

- **Carrier bag or nappy disposal bag,** to tidy away any accidents.

- **Change of clothes,** including a couple of pairs of trousers or leggings, several pairs of pants and even socks. It's incredible how far a little urine will go.

- **Plastic bag and towel for the car.** Car seat covers are washable, but it's easier if you don't have to. As an alternative, you could choose disposable nappy mats, which are handy and avoid mess, although if your child is still a bit unpredictable and you have lots of accidents they may prove rather expensive.

- **Nappy pants.** Keep these in reserve for those moments when you and your child have had enough. They're also useful to pop on your toddler if she's tired and often falls asleep during car journeys.

Above Don't forget your essential emergency kit. Days out will be less stressful if you're prepared for any little leaks or accidents.

Cuddles and compliments

Children respond well to flattery. It's what psychologists call 'positive reinforcement' – by complimenting good behaviour, you encourage your child to repeat it. This works very well with potty training.

If your toddler does a wee or poo on the potty, give him a cuddle or a round of applause to show how well he's done. Don't go overboard, though – there's no need to get the whole family to gather round and join in the celebrations. If you're too effusive, your child might worry that you'll be cross if he has an accident.

Act positive

Toddlers are extremely proud of what they've produced and will often present you with a full potty, like an offering. If you can, it's better not to gag, or squeal 'Put it down, you'll drop it!' This is actually a good opportunity to congratulate your child and then take the potty to the toilet together, to empty it.

The aim is to ensure that your child associates going to the potty with positive, happy feelings. So, even if you're at the end of your tether and he has managed to miss the potty and cover the carpet yet again, try to stay calm (or at least pretend to do so). Reprimanding or scolding can decrease your child's confidence and make him feel negative about potty training, which simply leads to more accidents.

Older children

Star charts –- to which a star sticker is added each time the child successfully goes to the toilet – can be an incredibly successful incentive for older kids, especially those who have reverted to frequent accidents when they had previously been dry.

Treats

Some people recommend giving a treat, such as a sweet or chocolate, every time a toddler uses the potty. I'm sure this is highly successful, and my children are always open to a spot of bribery, but I

feel a bit uneasy about plying them with chocolate quite as often as they go to the potty. You could try using strawberries or other healthy snacks instead, but in fact the achievement of learning to use the potty, together with undying parental gratitude when your child actually makes it, is often sufficient reward in itself.

In addition, it does seem rather mean to withhold a treat because your toddler still hasn't mastered all the necessary complex skills to control his bladder. After all, he's not doing this to be naughty – it's a learning process, and accidents are an integral part of that. For a child, not receiving a sweet could seem an awful lot like punishment.

Above *Let her know that she has done well and that you are very proud of her.*

Now wash your hands

It's never too soon to get your toddler into good habits. It may be you who's been wiping her bottom, but it's still a good idea to encourage your child to wash her hands herself. However, anyone who has a child will know that this can be a very long, splashy and deeply frustrating process.

Above Teach them that a whole roll of toilet paper isn't needed for each bottom wipe.

A running tap equals water-play to most children and it's much easier to usher them quickly out of the bathroom. However, it's important to be consistent, and if your child can have a bit of fun and associate that with going on the potty, then so much the better.

Provide a step so that she can reach the sink – but make sure that she doesn't use it to get her hands on anything else! Put cleaning chemicals, mouthwashes and medications well out of reach. My children have always found that a loo-brush can make a great sword or fairy wand, so it's better to keep them away from little fingers.

Wiping bottoms

When your child is a little older, you can teach her to wipe herself. This will inevitably involve huge quantities of toilet roll in the early stages, so for the sake of the environment, your drains and your budget, it's sensible to show her how much to use and to keep an eye on her at first.

Little girls should be taught to wipe from front to back. This ensures that any bacteria from the back passage aren't wiped towards the opening to the bladder, which can lead to urinary infections.

Top 10 mistakes – and how to avoid them

No parent is perfect and I've certainly worked my way through a number (if not all) of these top ten mistakes in my time. But if you and your child are struggling with the whole potty-training process, this list can help to identify where you may be going wrong.

1 Losing your cool. Children are emotional sponges who will unerringly pick up on your verbal and non-verbal messages. So, if you seem angry or disgusted, they will too. Of course, no one can be a calm and reassuring parent all the time. Cleaning up poo or wee isn't high on anyone's list of favourite activities, and putting yet another load of soiled clothes in the washing machine can wear you down. But do try to make sure the message you're giving is that toileting is a natural process, accidents aren't the end of the world, and that the toilet and potty are there for when your child feels ready.

2 Working to your own timetable. He's starting nursery, you're about to have another baby, it's summer and potty training will be easier. You can find so many reasons to potty train your child when it's convenient for you. This can work well, if your child is also ready – but trying to rush him will only end in frustration and disappointment for both of you. Try to let your child set the agenda for learning to use the potty.

3 Making him sit on the potty for hours. It's tempting to sit your toddler on the toilet and encourage him to stay there until he does something. The logic is that if he's on the toilet for ages there's much less chance of an accident – but imagine the

Above Try to let your child set the toilet training timetable.

57

boredom and discomfort of sitting on a cold plastic potty or seat for long periods. This may encourage your child towards the infinitely preferable warm, damp nappy. Instead, let him sit on the potty for as long as he feels comfortable: you may encourage him to sit for a little longer if you read him a story or leave a picture book by the toilet.

4 Nagging. It's all too easy to fall into the trap of repeating 'Do you want to go?' all the time. You want to be helpful and remind him to go to the toilet, but try not to overdo it. My husband was almost at breaking point when our elder daughter was learning to use the potty – I must have prompted her to go on it every five minutes. I was frustrated, he was irritated, and my poor little girl must have wanted to scream at me to shut up. The occasional gentle prompt is quite sufficient, although you can launch into action if your child appears to be about to go imminently.

5 Being inconsistent. At the risk of repeating myself, I'm going to bang the drum for consistency yet again. Your child needs to get the same message from you every time, and if he is sometimes allowed to do a wee in his nappy pants because you say it's okay, it will be difficult for him to understand that it's unacceptable on another occasion.

6 Going over the top. Children aren't stupid. If your toddler notices that every time he ventures near a potty you are at his side encouraging and applauding him, he will do it more and more. This can be fantastic, because it will improve his chances of learning to use the potty, but it can also become a trick to gain your attention. If trying to do a poo makes you stop what you're doing and concentrate on him, your child may well throw in a few 'false alarms'. Try instead to encourage him in a calm and controlled way, and congratulate him if he manages to go on his own without any help from you.

Above Sitting on a potty is cold and boring, let him do his business and go.

7 **Cutting down fluid intake.** In the beginning your child needs to go for a wee frequently to get the hang of it, so plenty of fluids are advisable. In addition, good hydration will help to prevent constipation, which can cause serious potty-training problems. Hard motions are painful to pass and your child may prefer to hold on, which makes the problem worse.

8 **Starting too soon.** Having your child out of nappies before his second birthday does not make you a good parent; similarly, you are not inadequate if your child is not potty trained by the age of 3. The only good reason for starting toilet training very early is because your child is ready.

9 **Putting it off.** Now I can hear you screaming: first she says not to do it too soon, and now she's telling us not to put it off. When is the right time? Relax: I'm not suggesting that there is a minuscule window of time in which the moment is precisely right to potty train. However, if your child is asking to go to the potty, wanting to wear pants and aware when he is weeing or pooing, it is sensible to get on with it. If you dismiss these signs, then your child will become used to ignoring the messages that his body is sending him and it may take longer for him to learn to use the toilet in the future.

10 **Never surrendering.** You need to know when you and your toddler have had enough. If you find yourself getting angry or frustrated, or your child seems very resistant, then it is probably a sign that you both need time out. It's better to wait until you've both regained your patience and enthusiasm. It's also better to take a breather if your child becomes constipated (if he has large or hard stools, or goes less than three times a week). In this instance, talk to your family doctor about increasing fibre and fluids in his diet, and then try again.

Above Plenty of fluids will make potty training much easier.

troubleshooting

4

I hate pants:
questions and answers

Q We've been trying to potty train our 3-year-old daughter for six months. She's been getting worse and worse, and now she often refuses even to sit on the potty. Is there something wrong with her?

A There's almost certainly nothing wrong with your little girl: she's just resistant to potty training. It can happen because she started trying too soon, or because she felt under pressure to use the potty and began to get negative feelings about it. It's a difficult and stressful process and all of us make mistakes; the problem is that once we've started it can be difficult to know when to give up or change direction.

It may be a good idea to take a little time out and put her back in nappies for a while. Have a chat with your daughter, maybe at bedtime when you are both calm and she's safe in a nappy, and see what she thinks. She may feel glad to have a rest from all the difficulties of potty training, in which case you can go back to it in a few weeks. If, however, she really wants to stay in pants then you can try again – but this time make sure she's the boss.

• **Let her take charge.** Tell her that she is a big girl and she is now in charge of going to the potty, although you'll help her whenever she wants.

• **Stop nagging.** Don't remind her to go: she hasn't responded to pressure in the past, so it's time to try a different strategy.

- **Applaud success and ignore accidents.** Congratulate her when she goes on the potty, and if she manages a whole day clean it may help to reward her with a special treat. Don't punish any accidents – pretend you hardly notice them. Children seek out attention, even when it's negative, so by ignoring the bad stuff you're encouraging the good.

- **Give her choices.** If she refuses to go on the potty, give her options. Suggest trying the toilet, a different potty or a potty in a different place. It'll make her feel in control and also gives her a way out of a confrontation without losing face.

- **Record her achievements.** Make a calendar or chart to show how well she's doing, and don't forget to fill it in when she's doing really well and you start to feel complacent.

- **Don't leave her wet.** If you leave your child in wet clothes she'll get used to it and it will cease to bother her. Encourage her to change if she has an accident and help her if she needs it.

- **Seek help.** If you feel you need it, there are professionals who can help you – your health visitor should be your first port of call.

Below Give her plenty of cuddles and compliments when she's doing well.

When should I be worried?:
questions and answers

Q My son has been dry for six months but insists on using a nappy to do a poo. He just won't do it on the potty.

'Poppy always had to have a nappy on to do a poo; she wouldn't go on the toilet. We managed to overcome the problem by sitting her on the potty after lunch every day. I'd spend 20 minutes on my own with her, chatting or reading a story. After a few days she did a poo – she was so relaxed it didn't seem to worry her, and she hasn't asked for a nappy again.'

Camille, mother of Poppy (6), Sophia (5) and Josh (4)

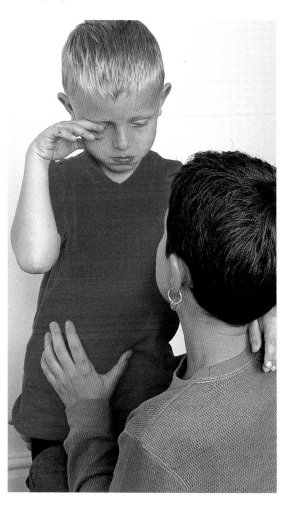

Right Toilet training can be frustrating for both of you.

A This is a common problem. Children see their stool as an extension of themselves and don't want to 'let it go'. They especially don't like doing it on the toilet because it seems to fall away from them, and they hate the big splash! The good news is that your son is obviously aware and in control of his bowels, because he requests a nappy when he needs to go. The Enuresis Research Campaign recommends getting him to stand in the bathroom and poo into his nappy. The next stage is to coax him onto the toilet to poo (still with his nappy on). Gradually you can remove the nappy, or even cut a hole in it, until he's ready to go without. This process can take a long time and be very frustrating – it's important to be firm but really encouraging, and to praise any small successes.

If this doesn't appeal, another method is to utilize a physiological phenomenon, the gastro-colic reflex. The bowel is stimulated to pass a motion after the stomach is distended with food. Choose a regular time, after a meal, when you will be able to sit with your child reading, talking or even blowing bubbles. The idea is to make him comfortable on the potty and his incentive is having a fun time with you. If you do this daily, in time your child may go on the potty and overcome his aversion.

Above Even though you child is happy to use his potty for a wee, he may be reluctant to use it for a poo.

Above *Fruit and fluids will help prevent painful constipation.*

Q **My 5-year-old daughter keeps on soiling her pants, she seems to refuse to go for a poo. What can I do?**

A The most common cause of soiling in children is chronic constipation. In some ways it seems illogical: the child appears to be pooing constantly, so how can she be constipated? It is easy to think that she is simply misbehaving or being lazy. In fact, hard lumps of poo are stuck in the back passage and softer stuff, from higher up the bowel, leaks around the edge, soiling the pants.

There are a number of causes including problems during potty training, a child being afraid to use the toilet at school, an illness, bullying or emotional stresses at home. It can be very distressing having a child that soils and it is important to reassure and support your daughter. She is not doing it on purpose, or because she can't be bothered to go to the toilet.

There are a number of ways to help ease the problem:

- **Get the diet right.** A diet that is rich in fruit, vegetables and fibre will help beat constipation. Children love grapes and baked beans, which are fantastic fibre providers. Make sure they're washed down with plenty of fluids.

- **Talk about it.** Chat to your child, reassure her that you're not cross and try to find out if she has any worries. Maybe she doesn't like doing a poo at school on her own, or it could be as simple as preferring the toilet paper at home.

- **Make it regular.** Encourage your child to sit on the toilet for a short time every day, preferably after a meal. You could use the time to practise her reading with her, or to chat about her day. It is possible to train the bowel by regularly sitting at the same time, although it's important that she doesn't strain.

- **Tell her she's a star.** Encourage and reward any successes – a poo on the toilet, or a day without soiling.

- **Consult your doctor.** They can help to diagnose the problem, by means of a simple examination (invasive investigations are seldom necessary) and exclude any rare anatomical causes of soiling. They can also prescribe medication – usually in the form of laxatives and stool softeners – provide support, and refer your child for specialist help if appropriate.

Right Your daughter may have difficulties when she's potty training, but with your help she can do it.

'Every day when my son came back from nursery I was afraid to look in his bag. I knew it would be full of soiled pants. He seemed happy and unaffected by his accidents, but I was anxious, upset and embarrassed, so much so that he used to try to reassure me, saying, "It's all right Mummy, don't worry, we've lots more pants at home."

But I was worried, very. He was due to start school and children can be terribly cruel – I could imagine them calling him names and leaving him out of playground games.

My son suffered from constipation, which I can trace back to when he'd had a fever about a year earlier. He ate and drank very little and passed one very hard stool, which caused a small tear in his bottom. It was excruciatingly uncomfortable and he decided that holding on and never going to the toilet again was preferable. So, he became constipated, held on more, and the whole frustrating cycle was set in motion.

I knew that the way I was dealing with the situation was hopelessly inadequate. As my son felt the urge to go to the toilet he became red faced and stood poker straight, his legs tightly squeezed together. Initially I tried to cajole him to sit on the toilet, but as he screamed and refused I found myself becoming increasingly frustrated and started shouting at him. Toilet time became a battlefield. One day I had cleaned up so many pairs of filthy pants that I was horrified to find myself shouting, "Look at these pants, they're disgusting – Mummy is very, very cross with you." We both cried that day. I felt so guilty; he was frightened and confused, and I didn't know how to help.

For a long time I'd felt too embarrassed to go to the doctor because I was sure it was my fault that my son had this problem, but I was at the end of my tether. He was really helpful, explained what was going on, gave him medicine to soften his stools and told me what foods would help. Things are improving – he still takes the laxatives, but I feel we're getting on top of the problem. I just wish I'd looked for help earlier.'

Sally, mother of Ben (5)

Q My son is 3½ and shows absolutely no interest in potty training. We haven't really started trying, because if we take his nappy off he'll just have an accident. How long should we wait before seeking help?

A Perfectly bright and happy children can be very slow to potty train and I certainly wouldn't be concerned until well after the age of 3. Slow potty training can run in families and boys do tend to be slower than girls, so there's no cause to panic. However, by 3½ I would recommend starting to try taking his nappy off and putting him on a potty regularly, following the advice given in chapters 2 and 3. You may find that he surprises you and takes to it fairly quickly. If not, it would be worth consulting your health visitor or doctor for an assessment and some advice. If your child is not potty trained by the age of 4 he should be referred to a specialist.

Right Even bright and happy children can be slow to potty train.

The toilet monster:
questions and answers

Q My 3½-year-old daughter still uses the potty all the time, I'd like her to try the toilet, but she just screams if we put her on it.

A Many children find the toilet scary – whether it's the noisy flush, the splashing water or the dragon their brother said lives at the bottom. Of course it's much more pleasant for us to flush the toilet instead of cleaning out a dirty potty, but a toilet can seem very big to a little child and it's important not to rush or force your daughter into making the transition. Try to introduce her to the idea gently using some of the suggestions below.

- **Put her potty right next to the toilet.** She'll get used to sitting on her potty in the bathroom and will become familiar with the toilet.

- **Let her watch you sit on the toilet.** If she seems happy, encourage her to help you flush when you have finished.

- **Place a safe step or stool next to the toilet.** It will help her climb up to use the toilet and form a safe platform on which to plant her feet, so that she feels secure.

- **Buy a child's toilet adaptor ring.** This fits onto the adult toilet and makes it seem less intimidating and more child-friendly.

- **Avoid flushing the toielt when she's sitting on it.** The noise and splashing can be terrifying for a little one.

Above *A step can make the toilet seem safer and less scary.*

70

- **If the splashes scare her, line the inside of the toilet bowl with toilet paper.** This absorbs some of the noise and splashing, and lots of children find that weeing away the paper can be a fun and distracting game.

- **Remember that when she first starts to sit on the toilet her little hands will get everywhere.** Try to keep the toilet as clean as possible, and supervise hand-washing afterwards to make sure that she's concentrating on her hands and not just giving the bathroom floor a good soaking.

- **Once she seems totally comfortable and secure using the toilet, quietly put the potty away.** You'll probably find that she won't even notice – she's a big girl now and doesn't need the potty any more.

Right Keep it clean – little hands can get everywhere.

71

'Jack hated flushing the toilet. Eventually we started saying that his poo was going to meet all his friends, the other poos, down the toilet. He found the whole idea very exciting and imagined them all having a party at the bottom of the toilet. It may sound bizarre, but it was the only thing that worked for us.'

Anna, mother of Jack (4)

Q My son gets really upset when I flush away his stools. What am I supposed to do? I can't just leave them in the potty.

A Some children see their motions as almost a part of them. Strange though it seems, flushing them away can be frightening and upsetting, especially combined with the noisiness of the toilet and the way it seems to 'gobble things up'. There are several ways of approaching this very common problem.

- Try rationalizing the whole thing and explaining what the waste is and where it's going when you flush the toilet.

- Sneak off to the bathroom and flush it all away when your toddler is distracted by something and (hopefully) he won't notice that you've done it.

- The final method, and in my opinion the most successful, is to turn the whole thing into a game. Encourage your child to wave and say 'Bye bye' to his poo as it disappears around the U-bend. You may get some strange looks in public toilets, but you'll have a happy child.

Relapses:
questions and answers

Q My son was totally dry and has just started having accidents again. It doesn't seem to bother him, but it's driving me mad. What should I do?

A Children start to have more accidents for lots of reasons. They are very sensitive to what's going on around them and a new baby in the family, a house move or a holiday can set them back. If you're running short of patience or feel that you may lose your cool, then consider taking a break from potty training for a short while and starting again when you've both had a breather. Sometimes you can both fall into bad habits and it can help to return to stage one and start again. Are you expecting too much of him at this early stage? Relapses often happen when parents leave the toileting up to their toddler before they're really able to cope alone.

If you are still struggling, or if your child seems unwell, it's worth consulting your doctor in order to rule out a physical cause of a relapse, such as a urine infection or constipation.

Right *A new baby in the family can lead to relapses.*

Q My daughter will not go for a wee until she is so desperate that she often has an accident. She denies that she needs to go, although it's obvious that she does. What can I do?

A In my experience, girls are particularly prone to this. They can be quicker to potty train, but once they get the hang of it they become convinced that they can hang on forever. As you've probably noticed, nagging your child constantly to go for a wee has little effect – she's often just too interested in what she's doing and worried that by leaving the room for a minute to do a wee she'll 'miss out' on something. She will grow out of this rather tiresome phase, but in the meantime you could try the following:

● **Take her with you when you go to the toilet.** If you go with her then she won't feel that she is missing something.

● **Use a star chart.** She is in full control of her actions, and by rewarding her if she doesn't have an accident you may encourage her to head off to the potty a little earlier.

Left If she is engrossed in a game she may 'forget' to go to the toilet.

Special needs:
questions and answers

Q My son has special needs. How will I know when the time is right to potty train him, and what should I do?

A The same principles and methods of potty training apply to all children. With a child who has special needs the process may take longer and, like all families who are embarking on the potty-training process, you and your son will need patience and support.

It's advisable to talk through the process with your doctor and any support workers you see regularly. They can help you to identify when your son has reached the level of development needed to perform each of the complex, interconnecting tasks that are required to use the potty. It can help to keep records, so that you can identify any patterns – such as the interval between eating and his bowels opening, for example.

In order be successfully toilet trained, a child needs to be able not only to recognize the need to go, but also to wait and get to the toilet, undo his clothes, pull down his pants and sit on the potty. It will help if you and your son's care workers look at each task and see whether he can achieve it, before planning to start potty training.

So, try not to rush – and remember to make the most of the help available to advise and support you and your son.

Above *All families embarking on potty training need lots of patience and support.*

dry nights

5

When to throw the nappies away

Even after successfully potty training your child, you're unlikely to be able to wave goodbye to nappies straight away. The majority of children aren't ready to be dry at night until at least the age of 3, and many take longer. As with potty training, every child is different and the tendency towards early or late dryness has very little to do with intelligence or other aspects of his future development.

'As soon as Mia, my first daughter, was potty trained, she started waking up in the night to go to the toilet. She was still very young and woke every four hours for a wee. It was exhausting – like having a new baby again. All my friends were trying to get their children out of nappies and I was desperate to get her back in! Fortunately, she's lasting a bit longer now, but I know that I won't be pushing my other daughter out of nappies in a hurry.'

Victoria, mother of Mia (6) and Sophia (3)

Don't rush your child out of nappies: there is little point in trying for dry nights until he's totally reliable during the day. If he's still having frequent accidents, then it's too much to expect him to get up, find the potty and go for a wee when he's half asleep.

Recognizing the signs

It's probably wise to allow a few months for your child to consolidate all he's learned about daytime dryness before moving onto the next stage. In general, between the ages of 3 and 4 is a good time to try your child without a nappy at night, although some may be ready much earlier. Signs that your child may be ready include:

- **His nappy is dry when he wakes in the morning.** Bladder capacity increases greatly between the ages of 2 and 4, so that children may be able to last most, or even all, of the night without going for a wee.

- **He wakes in the night and asks to go for a wee.** Some children notice the urge to pass urine even when they're asleep and wearing nappies. If this is the case, then it's time to try without.

- **He tears his nappy off in the night.** Toddlers who are used to lightweight, dry pants may become uncomfortable in a warm, soggy nappy and rip it off while they're asleep. If this is happening regularly to your child and you've had a few wet beds because of it, it may be worth trying him without nappies, or using nappy pants as an alternative.

- **His nappy leaks in the early morning.** As your child's bladder capacity increases he will pass much larger volumes of urine in one go. This can be too much for even some of the heavyweight night-time nappies to cope with, leading to leaks. Often this wakes your child and stimulates him to go to the potty himself.

- **He is keen to try without nappies.** Children usually know when they are ready to try without nappies. If he thinks he's ready and he's motivated to try, then don't stop him.

Above *If her morning nappy is dry it may be time to try without.*

Helping your child

If you think your child may be ready to face sleeping without nappies, you can help her to stay dry. With a little groundwork and guidance, you can prepare her – and the bed – for the night ahead.

- **Talk it through.** Have a chat with your child about whether she wants to try without a nappy. If she does, then choose a night when you've nothing important on the next day and explain what's going to happen.

- **Cover up.** Be prepared for a few wet beds. Make sure there are clean sheets and pyjamas to hand, and buy a mattress cover to protect against any puddles. Nappy mats can be used over the sheets in the early days, so that you don't even need to change the bedding, but beware: children tend to move in the night and their bottoms often wriggle off the position where you carefully placed the mat.

- **Be positive.** Congratulate your little one every time she wakes with a dry bed. The rate at which children achieve night-time dryness varies greatly: some start with only one or two dry nights a week and gradually build up over a number of months, whereas others are fairly dry straight away. If she does have an accident, try not to be cross. Changing wet sheets in the middle of the night can sap your energy and patience, but it's as frustrating for your child as it is for you, and she's not doing it on purpose – honestly.

- **Light the way.** Some children can't make it through a whole night without going for a wee.

'We had a real breakthrough when we put a nightlight and potty in Alice's room. It gave her the security and confidence she needed, and she's been dry at night ever since.'

Xanthe, mother of Alice (4)

Try leaving a nightlight in her room so that she can see her way to the potty. She may go on her own, but some children will want the comfort and reassurance of having you with them. Try to grin and bear it – her bladder capacity will gradually increase and she'll soon be able to sleep through.

- **Drink up.** It makes sense not to encourage your child to drink vast volumes of liquid just before bedtime. However, it is also important not to restrict a child's fluids. Dehydration can make the urine highly concentrated and this may irritate the bladder. This in turn means that the bladder is stimulated to pass urine at smaller volumes, making your child prone to night-time and daytime wetting.

- **Last thing at night and first thing in the morning.** Try to ensure that your child empties her bladder just before going to bed and, as most accidents happen first thing in the morning when the bladder is reaching capacity, encourage your child to have a wee as soon as she wakes.

Left Encourage him to drink to keep his bladder healthy.

Lifting

Lifting involves carrying your child to the toilet, gently talking to him and sitting him down to go for a wee. Usually he will be aware that he is emptying his bladder, but still sufficiently drowsy to go straight back to sleep. Parents and potty-training experts are divided on the subject of lifting. Most specialists advise against it, but many parents still do it – in secret!

'My son regularly used to need to go to the toilet at 3am. Sometimes he would wake up, sometimes he wet the bed and, often, once he was awake it would take an hour or so to get him back down. My husband and I were totally exhausted, so we started lifting him at 10pm when we went to bed. It seemed to work: he managed to last until 7am and we had unbroken nights. After a couple of months, we'd had a few glasses of wine and forgot to lift him – and he slept through. I think his bladder is a bit bigger now and the lifting was a way of getting us through that difficult time.'

Susie, mother of Jake (8)

The first few years of parenthood are characterized by chronic sleep deprivation. Lots of parents are so utterly exhausted that they will try anything for a good night's sleep. Lifting can seem like the answer and certainly help your child to sleep through the night without any accidents. However, experts believe that lifting your child will prevent him from learning to wake when he recognizes the signals that his bladder is full.

I confess that I lifted both my children – it was the only way we could reliably have undisturbed nights, and I chose the easy option. It worked for us: my daughters felt a great sense of achievement because they woke up with a dry bed, and we felt a lot less tired. After a few months we had a test night without lifting them, they slept through and, bar the occasional little accident, we've had no problems ever since.

If you are going to try lifting, talk to your child as you pick him up, explain what's happening and make sure he is aware that you are taking him to the toilet.

Ask the expert

'I discourage lifting because most parents don't wake the child. So, effectively you are teaching them to void while they are asleep. By lifting, parents are unwittingly encouraging bedwetting. However, it is always important to be sensitive to the needs of the family and I recognize that lifting can provide a much-needed rest from a stressful situation.'

Richard Butler, clinical psychologist and enuresis (bedwetting) expert

Below *If you decide to lift your child, talk to her and explain what you will be doing so that she understands what will be happening.*

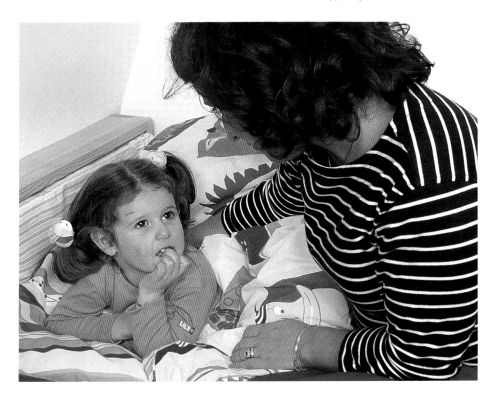

Bedwetting

The majority of children become dry on most nights by the time they are around 5 years old, although a number of children may still need to be lifted to achieve this (see pages 82–83). However, a great many children still struggle to stay dry at the ages of 6, 7 or even older. Bedwetting is particularly common in boys, and some studies have shown that little boys are twice as likely to wet the bed as girls.

Very few parents talk about this problem, so it can feel as if you are the only family suffering. The truth is that your child is far from alone. Bedwetting, or enuresis, often runs in families and research covering the UK, Ireland, the Netherlands and New Zealand shows that the numbers of children who regularly wet the bed average:

- 1 in 6 children aged 6 years
- 1 in 7 children aged 7 years
- 1 in 11 children aged 9 years
- 1 in 50–100 people over 15 years, including adults.

Further research suggests that the worldwide incidence of nocturnal enuresis for children aged 4 years and over ranges from 10 to 33 per cent. A total of around half a million children in the UK and between five and seven million in the USA frequently wet the bed.

Remember, your child and your family are not the only ones struggling to cope with this problem – there are lots of other people experiencing the same difficulties.

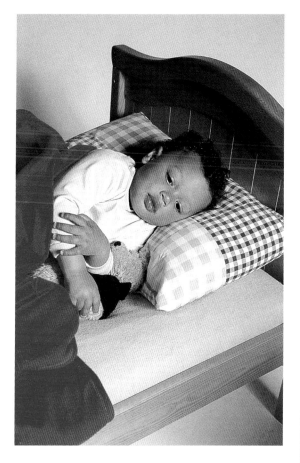

Left Bedwetting can become an embarrassing secret.

When is bedwetting a problem?

Bedwetting becomes more of an issue as children get older. Often, while a child is at home the family can manage, but as they increase in age they want to gain more independence, such as sleeping over at a friend's house or going on school trips. At this stage bedwetting can become an embarrassing secret, which can affect a child's school and social life. The good news is that help, support and good treatments are available.

Ask the expert

'I'd define bedwetting as a problem from 5 years of age. That's when we should consider looking into it further, seeing if there is anything causing it and giving advice. Most of the successful treatments start a little later, at the age of 6 to 7 years.'

Richard Butler, clinical psychologist and enuresis expert

Left An alarm
can wake a heavy
sleeper so that she
can get up to use
the toilet.

Strategies to try

1 **Go back to basics.** Although the research evidence for simple tactics such as lifting is limited, it may help your child have dry nights (see pages 82–83). This strategy can restore his self-esteem and confidence so that he can overcome this problem.

2 **Check the fluids.** As well as making sure that your child is drinking enough, it may help to monitor what he's drinking. Research has found that some fluids may make some children more prone to bedwetting. It may help to chart the last thing your child has to drink each day and check whether he wets more with juice, water or milk. The research is still at a relatively early stage, but these early findings may help your child to have a dry night.

3 **Try a star chart.** Charts to which star stickers (or an alternative reward) are added if a child is dry all night can be effective. I have had boy patients who coloured in pictures of their team's football strip. When a certain number had been coloured, they were treated to a day out watching their team with their parent, a tactic which was spectacularly successful. The trick is to make the rewards attainable, and never to punish accidents or mistakes.

Seeking advice

Talk to your doctor or health visitor. They can be an invaluable source of information and support. Most regions run bedwetting clinics, or have specialist advisors who can make sure there are no medical reasons for the bedwetting, and recommend and prescribe treatments.

Specialists believe that there are three main reasons why children wet the bed, and that different treatments are appropriate in each case.

1 **Heavy sleeper.** These children tend to sleep through and not wake in response to their body's signals that their bladder is full. Research has shown that the most effective form of treatment is an alarm. If a child is motivated and is at least 6 years of age, this can stop bedwetting in eight out of ten children. A bell or buzzer goes off as soon as a little urine starts to trickle out. This wakes the child (although it may help if you also go and help to wake her in the early days) and allows her to start to recognize the sensation that her bladder is full and she needs to empty it. Patience is needed, and the alarm should be used for around three months to be effective. Alarms may be prescribed by your doctor, school nurse or local specialist.

2 **Small bladder.** Some children may have a low capacity or irritable bladder, so that they are unable to go through a whole night without passing urine. As well as making sure your child is drinking enough fluids, your doctor may prescribe a drug treatment to stabilize the bladder and recommend a bladder-training programme during the day. This involves gradually extending the amount of time your child can 'hold on' for and so helps to increase the amount of urine that her bladder can hold.

3 **Hormonal problems.** The body secretes a hormone called vasopressin, which helps concentrate the urine. A drug called desmopressin can mimic this and ensure that less urine is passed at night. This is useful for one-off school trips and sleepovers, or as a welcome rest from constant bedwetting. It can also help the small number of children who may release too little of this hormone at night.

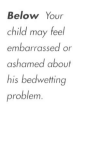

Below *Your child may feel embarrassed or ashamed about his bedwetting problem.*

'Thomas has always had problems with wetting the bed. As he got older, he got more and more embarrassed and wouldn't even talk to us about it. He used to get up and change his sheets and pyjamas on his own and then deny that anything had happened. It was absolutely heartbreaking for us. In the end, when he was 9, my brother had a word with him. He'd wet the bed quite a bit too, and I think the fact that his big, strong, clever uncle had had the same problem made it easier to bear. Thomas agreed to go to a special clinic and try an alarm. It was such a relief when he started to have dry nights. Now that he's dry most of the time, I can't believe how much his personality has changed as well. He's just so much happier and more confident. I really feel like I've got my little boy back.'

Sarah, mother of Thomas (10)

Top 10 tips for success

No one knows more about potty training than the mums, dads and carers who've been through it. Here parents and experts share their top tricks for trouble-free toileting.

I Treat children as individuals and don't push them too much. One of the children I look after was potty trained at 18 months while another is still in nappies at 3. I just try to wait until the individual child is ready.

Tanya Jolley, nanny

2 The most important thing is patience. Let the child be ready and then give plenty of loving guidance. It's a natural process, so try not to get uptight.

Vivienne Alderson, health visitor

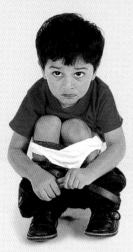

3 I had a potty with me wherever I went and would whip it out at the slightest opportunity. I kept it in a bag on the back of the buggy because in the early days they just can't hang on.

Min, mother of Polly (4), Esme (3) and Billy (1)

4 I think role models work brilliantly. With Oliver, I sent him for a wee with his hero, Henry, a bigger boy who was already potty trained. It helped him make the big step from weeing on the potty to doing it standing up at the toilet.

Sue, mother of Gemma (5) and Oliver (3)

5 We always put potties everywhere, in the living room, kitchen, bathroom and in the car. We worked on the principal that if they saw a potty they might remember to use it.

Tony, father of Megan (5) and Elin (3)

6 We made a big thing about going out to choose their first pair of pants. It was a real occasion. It was our way of showing them that they were big enough to stop wearing nappies.
Anna, mother of Alice (7), Amy (6) and Sam (3)

7 I tried to choose the summer months to potty train my kids – it just seemed so much easier. Their clothes are lighter, so they're easier to get out of and wash, and they used to have most of their accidents on the lawn. A few yellow patches of grass seemed a small price to pay for avoiding mopping up all those little puddles.
Alex, mother of Mia (9), Olivia (7) and Thomas (5)

8 We didn't do potties; we went straight to the toilet. I was very matter of fact about it and they picked up on that and were never frightened or worried. I kept a step close by, which helped them climb up and was useful for hand-washing, too.

Sarah, mother of Oliver (7), William (5) and Imogen (3)

9 From the beginning of potty training, when Jess was in nappy pants, I always took her to the toilet with me. I told her what I was doing and popped her on the toilet 'like Mummy'. I think it made her more prepared when she went into pants.

Debbie, mother of Jessica (3)

10 I think the best tip is to relax – after all, they won't be in nappies at 15, so they'll do it when they're ready!

Susie, mother of Charlie (3)

Index

Acknowledgements

All my thanks go to the organisations,
experts and parents who have helped
in compiling this book. In particular:
Jane McIntosh, Clare Churly, the
Enuresis Resource and Information
Centre (ERIC), the Encopresis
Information Exchange, the National
Childbirth Trust, Richard Butler and all
the mums, dads and carers who
shared their potty training experiences.
Finally, thanks to my husband for
looking after our little girls while I was
knee-deep in potties!

Executive Editor Jane McIntosh
Senior Editor Clare Churly
Senior Designer Joanna Bennett
Designer Bill Mason
Production Controller Viv Cracknell
Picture Librarian Jennifer Veall
Photography Peter Pugh-Cook
Stylist Aruna Mathur
with special thanks to
Babyjunction.co.uk

All photographs © Octopus Publishing
Group/Peter Pugh-Cook